To the good people of my adopted
community of Fairview, North Carolina.
—A.Z.

To my friends and family for
putting up with me all these years.
—G.C.

Contents

Gooder 'n Grits

The sayings, saws, and slogans from country folk—the down-home people of the farms, mountains, and ranges of America—are corny, clever, and colorful. There's almost always an element of truth in these beliefs from the backwoods and front porches, reflecting a way of thinking that can touch us all in different ways.

Conjured up during an era when our country was country, they have endured over time and offer us, in our frazzled techno-crazed 24/7 media-frenzied world, an opportunity to laugh and to ponder. As Maya Angelou once said, "Listen carefully to what country people call mother wit. In those homely sayings are couched the collective wisdom of generations."

We have collected hundreds of endearing, truthful, and amusing homespun adages and turns of phrases, and dozens of countrified jokes that we think will appeal to anyone who wants a change of pace in our pop culture–infused life.

Living in North Carolina's Blue Ridge Mountains for years — Gene is a born-and-bred Tar Heel — we and our families have learned to appreciate the way country folk paint their sentences in the most vivid and original analogies, sew simple words together into tapestries of truisms, and pepper their language with zesty wit. We've heard their sayings and laughed at jokes sprung from strange-sounding hollows, hamlets, and hinterlands. Real places like Possum Trot, Rabbit Hop, Pumpkintown, Tobaccoville, Licklog, Hardscrabble, Sodom, Climax, Matrimony, Trust, Tick Bite, Lizard Lick, Toast, Fig, Snapfinger, Bucksnort, Goose Hollow, and Bear Wallow.

It's not just in North Carolina that you can find expressive phrases, metaphors, and axioms. You can hear them in the accented voices of folks from Appalachia to the Adirondacks, from the cornfields of Illinois to the rangelands of Texas, from the forests of the great Northwest to the deserts of the sprawling Southwest. Country sayings are as varied as America itself and part of our national heritage. Best of all, they're just fun to read as all get out.

We hope that for you, reading this collection of country sayings and jokes is gooder 'n tupelo honey over hot grits.

—Allan Zullo and Gene Cheek

Consequences

- - - - - - - - -

Don't let your mouth write checks
that your rear end can't cash.

Inaction

- - - - - - - - -

You'll sit a long time with your
mouth wide open before a roasted
chicken flies in.

Putting on Airs

Even if you are in high cotton,
don't get above your raisin'.

Wishful Thinking

Wish in one hand, spit in the other,
and see which one gets full faster.

Excuses

Excuses are like backsides—
everybody's got one.

Revenge

- - - - - - - - -

Two wrongs don't make a right,
but they sure do make it even.

Owning Up

- - - - - - - - -

The easiest way to eat crow is
while it's still warm, 'cause
the colder it gets, the harder
it is to swallow.

Facing Reality

You can put your boots
in the oven, but that don't
make 'em biscuits.

A Light at the End of the Tunnel

The country doctor arrives at a cabin with no electricity in a hollow so deep they have to pipe in the sunshine. Inside are Fester and his wife, Tweetie, who's about to squeeze out their first baby.

During the delivery, the doc asks Fester to hold the lantern close to Tweetie so he can see. Soon, out pops the infant. Fester starts to put the lantern down when the doc hollers, "Wait a minute, hold that lantern back up here, Fester. There's another baby a-comin'!" Sure enough, Tweetie delivers a second infant. Fester goes to place the lantern on the table when the good doctor yells out, "Well, pick my peas! Here comes another one!"

Fester is swooning from the news. "Doc," he says, "you reckon it's the light that's attractin' 'em?"

Lies

If you pile up too many lies, the ground will be so steep you'll skin your nose climbin' up 'em.

Unnecessary Risks

Don't hit a hornets' nest with a short stick.

Compliments

Sayin' somethin' nice makes the old feel young and the poor feel rich.

Deceit

- - - - - - - -

Twistin' the truth is like puttin'
perfume on a pig.

Restraint

- - - - - - - -

If you're outnumbered, best keep
your mouth shut, or they'll tear
your butt up like a tater field
that's just been plowed.

Adversity

- - - - - - - -

What doesn't kill you makes
you stronger.

Seeking Advice

- - - - - - - -

Never ask a barber if he thinks
you need a haircut.

Self-Help

- - - - - - - -

If you want help,
look to the end of your arm.

Imperfection

Every dog ought to have
a few fleas.

Knowing Whom
to Criticize

Never smack a man chewin' tobacco.

Investing

The quickest way to double your
money is to fold it over and put it
back in your pocket.

Talking Dirty

A high-society lady was mortified when her daughter came home from college engaged to a young man with little money and no social standing. The dreaded day came when the haughty woman had to introduce her soon-to-be son-in-law to her friends. She winced as the young man talked to the snooty matrons in language that was neither grammatical nor refined. She couldn't have been more embarrassed if she had mistakenly served her guests moonshine instead of sweet tea.

The eyebrows of the hoity-toity were arched so high you could drive a team of horses through them. Rather than swoon in shame, the lady gritted her teeth and said to her daughter, who was still gazing starry-eyed at the ne'er-do-well, "Darlin', why don't you and your young man slip out to the kitchen and bring us some more cake?"

As the door closed behind them, Mrs. High-and-Mighty lowered her voice to her friends and said, "Well, you know, even the most fertile lands must be manured from time to time."

Inaction

- - - - - - - -

You'll never plow the field by
turnin' it over in your mind.

Guilt

- - - - - - - -

It's always the dirty dog
that howls the loudest.

Knowledge

- - - - - - - -

Live and learn
or die and know it all.

14

Excuses

- - - - - - - - -

Excuses are like armpits —
everyone has got at least two,
and they both stink.

The Company
You Keep

- - - - - - - - -

If you lie down with dogs,
you get up with fleas.

Ill-Gotten Gains

- - - - - - - - -

Honey is sweet, but don't
lick it off the briar.

Fake Compliments

- - - - - - - - -

Be careful you don't get
too sugary, or you'll drown
in your own sweet tea.

Advice

- - - - - - - - -

Don't give cherries to pigs
or advice to fools.

Wrong Impression

- - - - - - - - -

You can't tell the size of the turnips
by lookin' at their tops.

Anxiety

Worryin' gives small things
big shadows.

Opportunity

When life gives you scraps,
make a quilt.

Unwanted Relatives

Every garden has some weeds.

Promised Land

A Yankee decides to visit the grandest cathedral in each state. The first church he goes to is in California. Near the altar, he spots a golden telephone on a wall. Above it a sign reads, "$10,000 A MINUTE." The minister explains it's a direct line to heaven, so anyone who calls it can talk straight to God.

The Yankee visits cathedrals throughout the West, Midwest, and Northeast. Each time, he notices the same golden phone with the same sign. Each pastor, reverend, or priest tells him the same thing: It's a direct line to heaven.

On his first day below the Mason-Dixon Line, he enters a cathedral where, once again, he spots a golden telephone. But this time the sign reads, "25 CENTS PER CALL." He tells the pastor, "In every cathedral I've visited throughout this country, a call to God costs $10,000 a minute. How come a direct line to heaven from your golden phone costs only 25 cents?"

The pastor smiles and says, "That's easy. You're in the South now, so it's a local call."

Accountability

Don't blame the cow
when the milk goes sour.

Average Joe

We can't all be big shots.
Someone has to sit on the curb
and wave at 'em as they go by.

Unworkable Situation

There are times when the
big dog won't hunt.

Unintended Consequences

--- --- ---

Everyone loves the deer
'til it eats from the garden.

Ego

--- --- ---

Some people are so full
of themselves, you'd like to
buy 'em for what they're worth
and sell 'em for what they
think they're worth.

21

Telling Tales out of School

At Sunday dinner, Grandma Melba asked her grandson Buster what he learned in Sunday school that morning. He eagerly told the biblical story of how Moses led the Israelites to safety from the pursuing soldiers of the Pharaoh's army. Buster said that Moses used a golden megaphone to warn all the Israelites to flee Egypt. Then, according to the lad, "Moses hired engineers and real fast workers to build a bridge over the Red Sea. Once all the Israelites crossed over safely, Moses blew up the bridge, killin' all the Egyptian soldiers who were followin' 'em."

Grandma Melba nearly fell out of her rocker after hearing the tall tale. She leaned over and asked the boy, "Is that how your teacher told the story?"

"Not exactly," Buster replied, "but you'd never believe me if I told it her way."

Impossible Task

- - - - - - - - -

You can't make chicken salad
out of chicken feathers.

State of Mind

- - - - - - - - -

A good attitude is like kudzu —
it spreads.

Bar Fight

- - - - - - - - -

Pickin' a bar fight is like goin'
bear huntin' with a switch.

24

Wrong Assumption
- - - - - - - -

Just 'cause a chicken has wings
don't mean it can fly.

Liars
- - - - - - - -

Figures don't lie,
but liars figure.

Needless Worry
- - - - - - - -

Most problems ain't no bigger
than the little end of nothin'
whittled down to a fine point.

25

Ego
- - - - - - - -

Every crow thinks
he's the blackest.

Optimism
- - - - - - - -

There's a new day tomorrow,
and it ain't been touched yet.

Facing Reality
- - - - - - - -

If your cat had kittens in
the doghouse, would that
make 'em puppies?

First Impression

- - - - - - - - -

You can't tell much 'bout
a chicken potpie 'til you
cut through the crust.

Exaggeration

- - - - - - - - -

Don't let your mouth
overload your butt.

Criticism

- - - - - - - - -

Never insult an alligator
'til you've crossed the creek.

Family Problems

- - - - - - -

Every man needs to skin
his own skunk.

Making Matters Worse

- - - - - - -

When bugs throw a party,
they don't invite the chickens.

Sooner
Better Than Later

Great-granddaddy Floyd turned one hundred the other day, and all his kin gathered to toss him a mighty fine shindig. Floyd, who was all spiffed up, was still sharp as a tack and had all his acorns and all his teeth.

One of his great grandsons—the first to graduate from college—asked him, "Granddaddy, if you had to live your life over, would you make the same mistakes again?"

Taking a deep drag off his corncob pipe, Floyd replied, "I surely would, only I'd start a whole lot sooner."

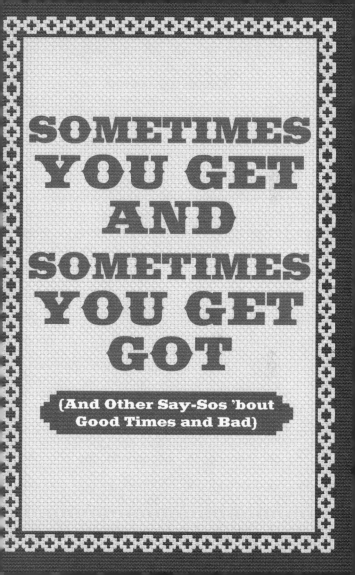

Feeling Good

- - - - - - - -

I feel finer than a frog's hair split
four ways and sanded twice.

*If you're in a really good mood,
you might say . . .*

If I felt any better, I'd be
two people.

Problems

- - - - - - - -

I got more problems than
I can say grace over.

*If your friend has a problem that she's
trying to ignore, you might say . . .*

If you got a rooster, he's goin'
to crow.

Blessed

- - - - - - - -

I'm so blessed, I could step
in manure and come out
smellin' like a rose.

*If you're referring to a friend who came
into wealth, you might say . . .*

Now, there goes a man who
broke out in money.

Ain't No Accidents

A wet-behind-the-ears insurance agent drives out to the farm of old man Grover, hoping to get him to renew his health policy. The young fellow finds Grover tuning up his tractor, but the farmer stops what he's doing to answer a few questions.

"Have you had any accidents in the past year?" the agent asks.

"Nope," Grover replies, "although that mule over yonder kicked in two of my ribs a while back, and last spring a rattlesnake bit my ankle."

"That's terrible," says the new agent. "Wouldn't you call those accidents?"

"Naw," the farmer replies. "I pretty much thought they did it on purpose."

Hard Times

I've fallen on stony ground.

If you want to offer hope to someone who's down in the dumps, you might say . . .

We've all seen sicker dogs
that got well.

Wealth

He's so rich, he buys a new boat
every time his old one gets wet.

*If you're well off, you might
want to boast . . .*

I'm richer than clabbered cream.

36

Poverty

I'm too poor to paint and
too proud to whitewash.

If you're always broke,
you might say . . .

Money thinks I'm dead.

Luck

Even a blind squirrel finds
an acorn now and then.

If you're talking about the luck of
the Irish, you might say . . .

He's so lucky, he could sit on a fence
and the birds would feed him.

Lip Service

Old codger Roscoe was sitting on the bench in front of the general store, whittling a gee-haw whimmy-diddle, when his friend Virgil arrived in a mule-driven wagon.

Virgil jumped off the wagon, tied the mule to a post, and then walked to the back of the animal, lifted up its tail, and planted a kiss smack dab on its rear end.

Roscoe dropped his whittling knife and said, "Did I just see what I just saw?"

Virgil nodded and said, "I reckon you did."

"Why would you do a durn fool thing like that?"

"I have a powerful bad case of chapped lips."

"And what you just did cures 'em?"

"Nope," said Virgil, "but it keeps me from lickin' 'em."

Poverty

I don't have a pot to pee in
nor a window to throw it out of.

If you're flat broke, you might say . . .

My piggy bank is as useful as an
ashtray on a motorcycle.

Good Fortune

I'm livin' on the lucky side
of the road.

*When things are going well financially,
you might say . . .*

I'm keepin' my smokehouse greasy.

Hard Times

- - - - - - - - - -

I'm so unlucky, I wouldn't hit
water if I fell out of a boat.

*If you're talking about someone
who's a little worse for wear,
you might say . . .*

Looks like he's on the backside
of hard times.

Down in the Dumps

Oakie was madder than a wet hen as he called over his four sons and yelled, "Which one of you goldurn sprouts pushed the outhouse in the river?"

No one said a word, so Oakie calmed down and said, "Years ago, when George Washington was a boy, he cut down a cherry tree. His pa asked him, 'George, did you chop down the cherry tree?' And George told him, 'I cannot tell a lie. Yes, I did.' His pa didn't punish him 'cause he told the truth. So I ask you once again: Who pushed the outhouse in the river?"

His youngest son stepped forward and confessed, "It was me, Pa."

Oakie threw him over his knee and whaled the daylights out of him. The little boy looked at Oakie through tear-filled eyes and whined, "You said George Washington wasn't punished for confessin' he chopped down the cherry tree."

"That's true," said Oakie. "But when that happened, his pa wasn't sittin' in the tree."

Happy Days

- - - - - - - - -

If times get any better, I'll have
to hire somebody to help me
enjoy 'em.

*If you're feeling extremely joyous,
you might say . . .*

I'm as happy as a calf in clover.

Life

- - - - - - - - -

One day you're drinkin' wine, the
next day you're pickin' grapes.

*If someone's life took a turn for the worse,
you might say . . .*

One day you're the peacock, the
next day you're the feather duster.

Poverty

- - - - - - - - -

I'm so poor, I had to fry up
my nest egg.

*If you came from a poverty-stricken
childhood, you might say . . .*

We were so poor, my brother
and I had to ride double on our
stick horse.

Loyal Follower

Junior went up to his pop and announced, "Pa, I'm leavin' the hills to look for adventure, excitement, and beautiful women."

Junior went into his room and packed his meager belongings. As he turned to leave, his pop blocked the doorway, so Junior said, "Don't try to stop me, Pa. I'm on my way."

Holding up his own suitcase, his pop replied, "Who's tryin' to stop you? I'm goin' with you!"

Ups and Downs

The sun don't shine on the same
dog all the time.

*If you want to inject a little positivism
into a bleak situation, you might say . . .*

Even a barren apple tree gives you
some shade.

Short of Cash

There's too much month left
at the end of the money.

*If you're in a bad financial situation,
you might say . . .*

I'm so broke, I'd have to borrow
money to buy a drink of water.

Taking Chances

- - - - - - - - -

Sometimes you're the windshield
and sometimes you're the bug.

To a gambling man, you might say . . .

Sometimes you eat the bear,
and sometimes the bear eats you.

Luck

- - - - - - - - -

He attracts luck like a magnet
does a horseshoe.

*Talking about a guy who always comes
out ahead, you might say . . .*

He can slide down a hundred-foot
locust tree with a wildcat under
each arm and never get a scratch.

Poverty

I'm so broke, I can't pay attention.

*If you're a little short of cash,
you might say...*

If a trip 'round the world cost
a dollar, I wouldn't make it to the
end of the driveway.

Financially Challenged

I'm as poor as gully-dirt.

*If a friend asks to borrow money
from you, and you don't have any to lend,
you might say...*

You went to a goat's house
lookin' for wool.

Problems

- - - - - - - -

Every path has its puddles.

*If you're facing several problems
at once, you might say . . .*

I'm in a bad row of stumps.

Poverty

- - - - - - - -

I'm so poor, I can't afford
tears to cry.

*If you're short on cash,
you might say . . .*

There ain't a tater in the patch.

Dilemma

- - - - - - - -

I'm caught where the
wool is short.

*If you're trying to figure out which
of your problems to deal with first,
you might think . . .*

There ain't no difference
between a hornet and a yellow
jacket when they're both buzzin'
in your pants.

52

Bearing Down

Jethro took his wife and mother-in-law hunting way back in the hills. They spread out, looking for game. About sundown, Jethro found his wife, and the two went to collect his mother-in-law. All of a sudden, they heard the old lady screaming like a cat with its tail caught in the barn door. They rushed toward the sound, rounded a clearing, and came upon a chilling sight: the mother-in-law was backed up against a tree, face to jowls with a large, menacing bear.

"Jethro, what are we goin' to do?" wailed his wife.

"Be still," he told her. "That bear got hisself into this mess, let him get hisself out of it."

Great Fun

I'm havin' more fun than a
lost dog in a meat market.

*If you had a great time clogging at the
church dance, you might say . . .*

I sure tore up the pea patch.

Drinking

You're so drunk, you couldn't hit a
bull in the butt with a bass fiddle.

*If someone had too much to drink over
the weekend, you might say . . .*

You look like you've been
chasin' cars.

Chilling Out

I feel so lazy on the weekends that
I have to speed up just to stop.

*If you want to let things come as they
may, you might say . . .*

Charge it to the dust and let
the rain settle it.

Party Time

You look like you've been sackin'
wildcats and plumb run outta sacks.

*In response to someone who asks you to
join a wild party, you might say . . .*

I'll jump on that like a duck
on a june bug.

Long Hours

I'm workin' from can to can't.

If you're going to have a long day at work, you might say . . .

It'll be dark-thirty before
I get home.

Work Experience

The new broom might
sweep clean, but the old broom
knows the corners.

*If you're touting your work experience,
you might say . . .*

The older the fiddle,
the sweeter the tune.

58

The Boss

- - - - - - - - -

He's the big cheese in this trap.

If you're warning your co-worker against leaving his job early without the boss finding out, you might say . . .

That's like tryin' to slip sunup past a rooster.

Bait and Switch

A Yankee was fishing off the coast
of Florida when his boat capsized.
He wouldn't swim to shore because
he feared alligators, so he clung
to the hull. When he spotted a
cracker named Hump fishing off the
dock, the Yankee shouted to him,
"Are there any alligators in these
waters?"

Hump replied, "Nope. There
ain't been any in years."

The Yankee heaved a sigh of
relief and, believing it was safe,
he started swimming for shore.
About halfway there, he asked the
cracker, "How come there aren't
any alligators here?"

Answered Hump, "The sharks
ate 'em all."

Busy

- - - - - - - -

I'm as busy as a one-legged man
at a butt-kickin' contest.

*When someone asks if you're busy,
you might say . . .*

There ain't no flies on me.

Lazy Worker

- - - - - - - -

He'll never drown in his
own sweat.

*If you're referring to a nice
co-worker who is somewhat lazy,
you might say . . .*

He's a good dog, but he don't
like to hunt much.

61

Exhaustion

- - - - - - - - -

I'm so dog-tired, my butt's
draggin' out my tracks.

*If your body is telling you that you can't
work anymore, you might say . . .*

Just throw me in the chair and
call me a sack of taters.

Lazy Worker

- - - - - - - - -

He's always lookin' for
sundown and payday.

*If accused of being lazy,
you might say . . .*

I'm not afraid of work. I can lay
down right beside it and go to sleep.

Difficult Work

- - - - - - - - -

A hard job is like forty miles
of rough road.

*When facing a difficult task,
you might say . . .*

That ain't no hill for a climber.

Overwhelmed

- - - - - - - - -

I'm so far over my head, I have to
look up to see bottom.

*When you're swamped with work
and can't seem to get ahead,
you might say . . .*

I feel like a rubber-nosed
woodpecker in a petrified forest.

63

Gone Fishin'

Two country boys are at their special fishing hole when all of a sudden, the game warden jumps out of the bushes.

One of the boys throws down his rod and hightails it through the woods like a fox on fire, but the warden is hot on his heels. About a half mile later, the boy stops and stoops over with his hands on his thighs to catch his breath.

The game warden finally collars him and says, "Let's see your fishin' license, boy."

The lad pulls out his wallet and shows the warden a valid fishing license.

"Well, son," says the warden, "you must be dumb as a box of rocks. You have a license, so you didn't have to run away from me."

"I reckon not, sir," replies the boy, "but my friend back yonder, well, he don't have one."

Management

- - - - - - - - -

They think they know everythin',
but they're as lost as geese
in a snowstorm.

*If you're hassled at work by
management, you might say . . .*

I'm as harried as a stump-tailed
cow durin' fly season.

Told You So

"You don't want to do any business with that Jake," Elmer told his friend Trace. "He's slicker than a leaky oil pan. Heck, he could steal the buttons off the long johns you're wearin' and sell 'em back to you as rare coins."

"Ain't that the gospel," said Elmer. "Why, just last week, I was over at Jake's place, spittin' nails and carryin' on. I hollered, 'Jake, you no-good snake in the grass, that mule you sold me is half-near blind!'

"And Jake says, 'I told you before you bought him, he was a fine mule, but didn't look good.'"

Bad Boss

- - - - - - - - -

He's been chased through the forest
of mean and hit every tree trunk.

*If you're warning your co-worker not
to cross the boss, you might say . . .*

He'll get mad enough to run a
stray dog off a meat wagon.

Overworked

- - - - - - - - -

I'm so overworked, I'm busier
than a funeral home fan in August.

*When work is piling up,
you might say . . .*

I've got more tobacco
than I can chew.

Cheapskate Boss

He's so tight that when he blinks, his toes curl.

If you're complaining that your stingy boss won't give you a raise, you might say . . .

He's tighter than bark on a tree.

Doing Your Share

Them that don't pluck don't get chicken.

Referring to a co-worker who doesn't pull his weight, you might say . . .

They call him "Blister" 'cause he don't show up 'til the work is done.

69

Forcing His Hand

Luke was having a hard time living up to his promise to his wife not to drink any more corn liquor.

One day as he was driving back from town, he stopped and picked up a hitchhiker who was fixing to visit his granny. No sooner did the young man get seated in the pickup than Luke pulled a gun on him and ordered him to get the jar of moonshine out of the glove compartment. "Take a big swig," Luke said, waving the gun.

The frightened hitchhiker took a gulp and darn near gagged to death.

But he was shocked even more after what happened next: Luke handed him the gun and said, "Now you take the gun and force me to take a drink."

Busy

- - - - - - - - -

I'm always so busy you'd
think I was twins.

*If you're going to have a busy day,
you might say . . .*

I got so much to do, I've got
to work early 'cause early
don't last long.

Bad Boss

He's meaner than a fryin' pan
full of rattlesnakes.

*If your boss keeps yelling at you,
you might think . . .*

If you keep whippin' the horse back
into the barn, he'll finally kick you.

Hard Work

Grass don't grow on a busy street.

*If someone asks you the secret of your
success, you might say . . .*

Gardens ain't made by sittin'
in the shade.

73

Unfinished Work

- - - - - - - -

You need to go back to the
chicken pen and start scratchin'.

*If your co-worker is stalling over
completing a task, you might say . . .*

Time to paint your butt white
and run with the antelope.

Overwhelmed

- - - - - - - -

I feel like a short dog in tall grass.

*When a co-worker doubts that you can
get the job done, you might say . . .*

I ain't as good as I once was, but
I'm as good once as I ever was.

Good Worker

- - - - - - - - -

He can haul a sawed log
to hell and back.

*If you're describing a co-worker who
uses more brains than brawn,
you might say . . .*

A sharp ax is better than
big muscles.

Completing a Job

- - - - - - - - -

If you want the job done in time,
you better light a shuck.

*If you want to do a job in a perfunctory
fashion, you might say . . .*

We ain't got time to do it right,
so just hit it a lick and give it
a promise.

Busy

- - - - - - - - -

I'm busier than a set of jumper
cables at a family reunion.

*If you have too many things to deal with
at once at work, you might say . . .*

I'm weedin' a pretty wide row.

Big Shot

Otis staggered into the doctor's house and, pointing to his blood-soaked chest, said, "Hey, Doc, can you patch me up?"

"What happened to you?" Doc asked with alarm.

"My cousin Sully shot me."

"Why?"

"Well, me and the boys was havin' a good time drinkin', when Sully picked up his shotgun and said, 'Who wants to go huntin' with me?'"

"And then what happened?"

"I stood up and said, 'Sure, I'm game.'"

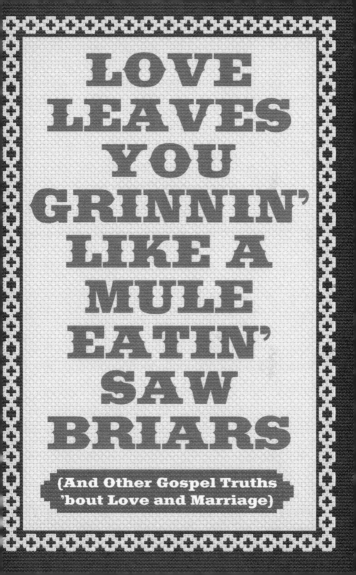

Unusual Choice
for a Spouse

- - - - - - - - - -

There's a lid to fit every skillet.

*If a friend married above his station,
you might say . . .*

He was raised on firebread and
soppin' gravy. She was raised
on ham and eggs.

Romance

If women were flowers,
I'd pick you.

*If you're in a romantic mood,
you might tell your honey . . .*

That moon is pretty enough to
make a rabbit smooch a hound dog.

Divorce

Looks like them two will end up
splittin' the blanket.

*If you're talking about the end of a
relationship, you might say . . .*

Breakin' up hits you up side the head
and leaves you down in the mouth.

Compliment

Well, don't you look prettier
than a pat of butter meltin' on
a short stack.

*If your honey asks, "How do you like
my new perfume?" you might say . . .*

You stink pretty.

82

Warning to Husbands

Don't buy anythin' with
a handle on it, 'cause it can
only lead to work.

*Talking about husbands trying
to understand their wives,
you might say . . .*

Any man tryin' to figure out
a woman ends up as confused
as a cow in a parkin' lot.

Magic Doors

On their first visit to the big city,
Dilbert, his wife, Deanna, and
their son, Dewey, enter a huge
department store for the first time.
Dilbert and Dewey walk around in
awe while Deanna goes off to shop
for some unmentionables.

Dilbert and Dewey are wide-
eyed by the wonders of the place,
especially by two shiny, silver walls
that move apart and then slide back
together.

"Paw," Dewey asks, "what's
that?"

Dilbert shakes his head. "I
dunno, son. I ain't never seen
anythin' like it."

While the two watch in amazement, an ugly, overweight woman waddles up to the moving walls and presses a button. The walls open and she steps into a small room. The walls close. Father and son watch the numbers above the walls light up: one, two, three, four. A few seconds later: three, two, one. Then the walls open up and out struts a stunning blonde so pretty that the sight knocks the clay right off of their boots.

Not taking his eyes off the beauty, Dilbert whispers to his son, "Dewey, go get your momma."

Marriage

Marriage is just like sittin'
in a bathtub. Once you get
used to it, it ain't so hot.

*If you're talking about the secret to a
happy marriage, you might say . . .*

Life is simpler when you plow
'round the stumps.

Hard-to-Please
Woman

She's so persnickety, she wouldn't
be happy in a diamond mine.

*Speaking about a wife who's extremely
fussy, you might say . . .*

When she gets to heaven,
she's gonna ask for better
accommodations.

Lousy Husband

- - - - - - - - -

He's the kind of man who tells his
wife, "I can't do all that work 'cause
I got a bone in my leg."

*Referring to a woman who married a
loser, you might say . . .*

She sure got the short end of the stick.

Living in Sin

- - - - - - - - -

Now, there's a couple that ate
supper before they said grace.

*If you admit that you had premarital
sex, you might say . . .*

We planted the corn before the
fence was built.

It's All Relative

Tommy Lee and Katy Lynn had been married just long enough for the new to wear off, so now they were getting under each other's skin. One day while they were driving to see her parents, they were arguing in the car. As they drove past a barnyard full of pigs and jackasses, Tommy couldn't resist saying, "Relatives of yours?"

"Yep," says Katy Lynn, without skipping a beat. "My in-laws."

Love-Struck

I'm as happy as a goat in a
briar patch.

*If you're talking about how deeply in love
you are, you might say . . .*

I'm as happy as if I had good sense.

Disagreements

Arguin' with her is like a bug
arguin' with a chicken.

*If your spouse says something
inflammatory during an argument,
you might think . . .*

That's puttin' the fat in the fire.

Compliment

You look prettier than a
store-bought doll.

*Referring to a beautiful woman,
you might say . . .*

She's prettier than a little red wagon
full of speckled pups.

Cursed

At the county fair, old man Homer slipped into the tent of the carnival fortune-teller and asked her, "Can you remove a curse I've been living with for the last forty years?"

The fortune-teller fingered the beads around her neck and studied Homer for a minute before answering, "Of course I can. But you have to tell me the exact words that were used to put the curse on you."

"That's not a problem," Homer declared. "I remember it like it was yesterday. The exact words were, 'I now pronounce you man and wife.'"

Two-Timer

- - - - - - - -

He's as low as a snake in
a wagon track.

*If your friend is trying to cover up his
affair after being spotted with his
mistress, you might say . . .*

You can hide the fire, but what're
you gonna do with the smoke?

Beautiful Woman

- - - - - - - -

I'd like to walk her to the front row.

*If you're talking about a woman who
ages well, you might say . . .*

She's a spittin' image of herself.

Flirting

Flirtin' with a married woman
is as safe as if you were in
Abraham's back pocket and
him fixin' to sit down.

*Warning your married friend about
flirting, you might say . . .*

It's like tryin' to lick honey off a
blackberry vine—it looks temptin'
but you're just gonna get all cut up.

94

Choosing the
Right Spouse
- - - - - - - - -

If you don't want blisters on your
butt, ride a good saddle.

*If you want to compliment a man on his
choice for a wife, you might say . . .*

You sure didn't pick up
no crooked stick.

Chatterbox Wife
- - - - - - - - -

She'd talk the ears off a dead mule.

*To a wife who can't stop talking,
you might say . . .*

You better stand up, 'cause you're
talkin' the legs right off your chair.

Advice and Consent

Sally Ann had sweet eyes for Billy Bob, who didn't have a clue that she was smitten with him. The two were walking down a path from his house. He was loaded down with a washtub on his back, a live chicken under his arm, and a cane in his hand that he was using to lead a calf.

When they came to the woods, Sally Ann hesitated. She fluttered her baby blues and said coyly, "Billy Bob, I'm afraid to walk in there with you 'cause you just might try to steal a kiss."

He shook his head and said, "With all that I'm carryin', how could I possibly kiss you?"

"Well," Sally Ann replied, "you could stick that cane in the ground, tie the calf to it, and put the chicken under the washtub."

Husband
of Few Words

- - - - - - - -

He don't use his kindlin'
to start a fire.

*Referring to a husband who
acts cool because he hides his
emotions, you might say . . .*

There may be snow on the roof
but there's fire in the hearth.

Philanderer

- - - - - - - - - -

Ask him no questions and he
won't tell you no lies.

*Referring to a friend who has fallen
for two women at the same time,
you might say . . .*

He's so confused, he don't know if
he's afoot or on horseback.

It Should Be
a Whopper

Junior climbed down from the
sleeping loft and tiptoed into his
parents' bedroom where his momma
was reading one of those dime-store
novels by candlelight.

"It's three in the mornin'," she
said. "What in tarnation are you
doin' in here?"

"I can't sleep, Momma. I was
hopin' you could tell me a story."

She patted her bed and said,
"Come and sit a spell with me,
honey. When your darn-fool daddy
comes home, he can tell us both
one."

Loveless Marriage

- - - - - - - - - -

She's as cold as a cast-iron
toilet seat.

*If you're not getting as much loving as
you want, you might say . . .*

I'm as frustrated as a rooster in
an empty henhouse.

Smooth Talker

- - - - - - - - -

Women need to keep him
at a distance—like they do
skunks and bankers.

*If women are swooning over a
slick operator, you might tell them . . .*

You might think he's the
genuine article, but he ain't
got no guarantee.

Great Catch for
a Husband

- - - - - - - -

He's bigger than life and
twice as handsome.

*If you're talking about a man who
dotes on his wife, you might say . . .*

He carries her on a silk pillow.

Love-Struck

- - - - - - - -

I'm as happy as a tick on a fat dog!

*If you're acting goofy because
you've fallen head over heels in love,
you might say . . .*

I'm so mixed up, I don't know
daylight from dark.

Depraved Woman

- - - - - - - - -

She's so bad, she can make a
preacher lay down his Bible.

*If you're talking about a woman with
loose morals, you might say . . .*

They call her "Radio Station,"
'cause any man can pick her up.

Morally Challenged
Husband

- - - - - - - - -

He ain't fit to roll with the hogs.

*If you and your divorced friends are
trashing your ex-husbands,
you might say . . .*

Good men are as scarce as deviled
eggs after a church picnic.

Lousy Husband

He's as sorry as a two-dollar watch.

If you're talking about your bar-hopping husband, you might say . . .

Keepin' him home at night is as easy as puttin' socks on a rooster.

Posted

One day the wife passes on and they prepare the coffin and put her in it. The pallbearers start to take her to the church, but when they're going through the yard gate, they bump the coffin against a post and the old lady sits up, wide awake. They carry her back in the house and she lives for another ten years.

Finally, she passes on for sure. They get out the coffin, put her in it, and again the pallbearers start for the church. When they get near the gate, her husband cautions, "Now, boys, watch out for that post."

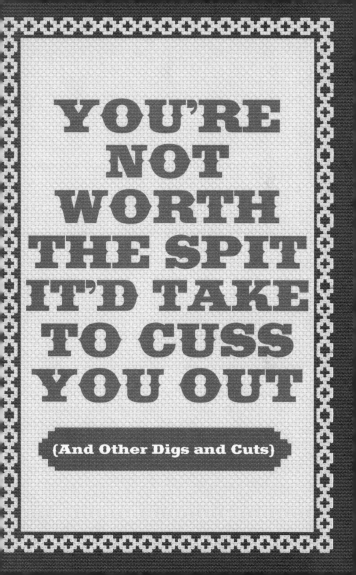

Dishonest

- - - - - - - - -

You lie so much, you have to hire
someone to call in your dogs.

Gossiping

- - - - - - - - -

You ain't nothin' but a trash toter.

Ineffective

- - - - - - - - -

You're as useless as a milk bucket
under a bull.

Confused

- - - - - - - - -

You couldn't find your
own butt with two hands and a
search warrant.

A Bunch of Bull

An old farmer filed a lawsuit against the railroad, claiming that the two o'clock freight train that clickety-clacked through his field every day had likely turned his prize bull into burger meat. All the farmer wanted was to be paid the fair market value for his missing bull.

On the day of the trial, this young hotshot big-city lawyer for the railroad sweet-talked the farmer into settling out of court for half of what he was asking.

After the farmer signed the release and got his check, the lawyer just couldn't resist gloating and said, "I hate to tell you this, old man, but there was no way I could've won the case. The engineer was asleep and the fireman was in the caboose when you lost your bull. I didn't have a single witness to put on the stand. I was bluffing you."

The farmer nodded and said, "I hate to tell you this, young man, but there was no way I could've won the case. That dadgum bull came home this mornin'."

Ignorant

If you put your brain in a matchbox, it would roll 'round like a BB in a boxcar.

Dishonest

You're so crooked, you could hide behind a corkscrew.

Vocally Challenged

You couldn't carry a tune in a bucket.

Lying

- - - - - - - - -

Your tongue wags at both ends.

Arrogant

- - - - - - - - -

You're so stuck up, you'd
drown in a rainstorm.

Ignorant

- - - - - - - - -

If your brain was leather,
it wouldn't make a saddle for
a june bug.

Undependable

- - - - - - - - -

You're so worthless, the tide
wouldn't take you out.

Corrupt

- - - - - - - - -

You're so dishonest, you'd steal
the lard out of a biscuit.

Lazy

- - - - - - - - -

You wouldn't catch your breath
if it didn't come natural.

Morally Challenged

You're as crooked as a hound dog's
hind leg and twice as dirty.

Stupid

If dumb were dirt,
you'd be 'bout an acre.

Pessimistic

You're so negative,
you'd depress the devil.

Double Whammy

A Yankee comes down to visit his country folks, so naturally they drag him to church and introduce him to the preacher. After the service, the preacher stands at the door and shakes hands with the congregation.

"Well, Lord have mercy!" he declares upon seeing the visitor with two black eyes. "You didn't have those shiners when you came in. What happened to you?"

The Yankee winces and explains, "You remember the large lady that stood in front of me during the song service?"

The preacher nods.

118

"Well," says the Yankee, "I noticed her dress was wedged, so I reached over and pulled it out. That's when she clobbered me in the right eye."

The preacher shook his head in sympathy. "So what happened to your left eye?"

"She slugged me again."

"Why?"

"She was so angry at me for what I'd done, I tried to wedge her dress back in."

Intolerant

- - - - - - - -

You're so narrow minded,
you can see through a keyhole
with both eyes.

Disorganized

- - - - - - - -

You're so mixed up,
you couldn't organize a drinkin'
contest in a brewery.

Complaining

- - - - - - - - -

You're so ungrateful,
you'd gripe with a ham
under each arm.

Lazy

- - - - - - - - -

If you had a third hand,
you'd need another pocket
to put it in.

Scruffy

You look like the dog has been keepin' you hidden under the porch.

Corrupt

You're so crooked, no one can tell from your tracks whether you're comin' or goin'.

Deceitful

You're lyin' like a no-legged dog.

Inept

You're 'bout as handy as a
back pocket on a shirt.

Spineless

You're nothin' but an empty sack.

Fibbing

You're fuller than a tick that's
been suckin' on a dog all day.

Face to Face

Ella Mae isn't any bigger than a
cornstalk in June and has a face
as sweet as a moon pie. But, oh,
Lordy, what a mouth on that child.

She was down at the five-and-
dime, and all out of sorts because
her momma wouldn't buy her new
shoes. While her momma was
trying on a dress, Ella Mae sat on
a bench outside the dressing room
and sulked like a puppy whose bone
was filched.

The pouty little girl began
making not-so-nice faces in the
three-sided mirror, when a refined
woman walked over to her and said,

"You're such a pretty little girl, you shouldn't make those terrible faces. When I was your age I was told that if I made an ugly face, it would stay that way."

As quick as a whip, Ella Mae retorted, "Well, you can't say you weren't warned."

Ignorant

- - - - - - - -

If you put your brain in a
hummingbird, it'd fly backward.

Lazy

- - - - - - - -

You're too lazy to open an
umbrella when it rains.

Annoying

- - - - - - - -

I wish you'd take a long walk
off a short pier.

If you bump into someone you don't like, you might say . . .

Anytime you happen to pass my house, I'd sure appreciate it.

◆ ◆ ◆

If someone is acting like a martyr, you might say . . .

Get down off that cross, 'cause someone else needs the wood.

◆ ◆ ◆

If you want to slam someone who judges others, you might say . . .

You need to clean up your own backyard before talkin' trash.

127

If you want to threaten someone,
you might say . . .

I'll knock a knot on your head
and dare it to rise.

♦ ♦ ♦

If a salesman is giving you a line,
you might say . . .

Our cow died last night,
so we don't need your bull.

♦ ♦ ♦

If you're annoyed about receiving advice
from a hypocrite, you might say . . .

I don't see no corn in your crib.

128

*If you're putting down someone
who's nothing but a big pretender,
you might say . . .*

You're all hat and no cattle.

◆ ◆ ◆

*To someone who takes way too much time
to complete a task, you might say . . .*

You'd be the right feller to send for
the doctor if the devil was sick.

◆ ◆ ◆

*If you want to threaten someone,
you might say . . .*

I'll cut off your water and
take out the meter.

129

A Tight Situation

Between slopping the hogs, weeding the beans, and chopping firewood, Luanne had no reason to wear fancy clothes. But every once in a while, she liked to get gussied up for the church socials and barn dances.

One day she came home with a fancy store-bought dress and put it on for her husband, Donny Joe, to admire. Now, when she wasn't in her dungarees, Luanne could show off more curves than a mountain creek. So, there in the bedroom, she wriggled into her new dress and asked Donny Joe, "What do you think?"

"I'm a little confused," he said.

"How so, Donny Joe?"

He answered, "Are you outside tryin' to get in, or inside tryin' to get out?"

To someone who is wild behind the wheel, you might say...

You're gonna cause a month's worth of buryins.

♦ ♦ ♦

To someone who acts arrogant after inheriting a large sum of money, you might say...

The higher a monkey climbs, the more he shows his butt.

♦ ♦ ♦

If you're knocking someone whose family has a history of lowlifes, you might say...

There're lots of nooses hangin' in your family tree.

*If you're annoyed by someone
who likes the sound of his own voice,
you might say . . .*

You've got a ten-gallon mouth
and an elephant's ears.

◆ ◆ ◆

*If you want to threaten someone,
you might say . . .*

I'll cloud up and rain
all over you.

◆ ◆ ◆

*To a person who thinks he's a big shot,
you might say . . .*

I knew you when you weren't,
and you still ain't!

133

Flying in the Face of the Law

A young country man named Jonas was driving his pickup, which was piled with manure, when he was pulled over by the sheriff.

"Boy, I'm writin' you a citation for carryin' too big of a load," said the sheriff.

As the lawman took out his pen, some of the flies accompanying the manure started to buzz him. He swatted and cussed at the flies.

"Them's circle flies," said Jonas. "We call 'em that 'cause back on the farm, they're always circlin' the horse's ass."

"Boy, are you calling me a horse's ass?" the sheriff growled.

"Oh, no, sir," said Jonas. "But you can't fool them flies."

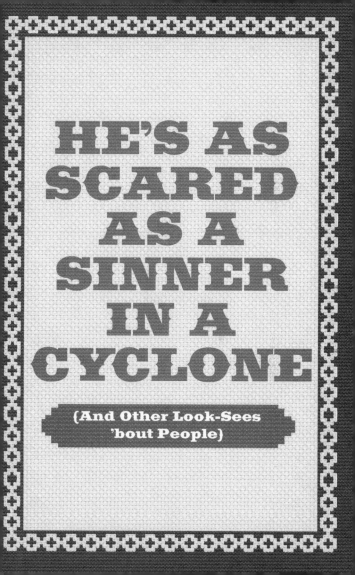

HE'S AS SCARED AS A SINNER IN A CYCLONE

(And Other Look-Sees 'bout People)

Intelligent

- - - - - - - - -

She's as smart as a tree
full of owls.

Lazy

- - - - - - - - -

It's a sorry dog that won't wag
its own tail.

Spirited

She's livelier than a puppy
with two tails.

Exaggeration-Prone

He's full of more nuts and berries
than a fat bear.

Unintelligent

He won't hurt his back
totin' his brains.

Arrogant

They're so snooty that if they
get to heaven, they're gonna ask
to see the upstairs.

Strong

He's tougher than a
one-eared alley cat.

Pompous

That big mouth is all vine
and no taters.

Untrustworthy

You can shake his hand,
but count your fingers when
you're done.

Brilliant

If his brain were a rifle,
he'd shoot the stinger off a bee.

Stupid

His cheese slid off his cracker.

Holding On

The family threw a surprise birthday party for Grandma Clara—a real shindig with cake and ice cream and balloons. At the party, her grandson Jimmy asked her, "How old are you, Memaw?"

"Forty-nine and holdin'," Clara answered.

Jimmy thought a minute and said, "Memaw, how old would you be if you let go?"

Contrary

If you throwed her in the river,
she'd float upstream.

Dishonest

He'd steal anythin' that ain't
too hot or too heavy to carry.

Open-Minded

She don't wear no blinders.

Brainless

He doesn't have as much sense
as you could slap in a gnat's butt
with a butter paddle.

Egotistical

She thinks she's the only
huckleberry on the bush.

Anxious

He's as jumpy as a cockroach
in a fryin' pan.

Honorable

- - - - - - - - -

He plows straight and to the
end of the row.

Sluggish

- - - - - - - - -

He was born tired and raised lazy.

Snooty

- - - - - - - - -

She wouldn't make a vest out
of God's own overcoat.

Dependable

- - - - - - - - -

He's all wool and a yard wide.

Chatty

- - - - - - - - -

She gets tuckered out from
her own chin music.

Stingy

- - - - - - - - -

He's tighter than the skin
on a sausage.

146

Uppity

- - - - - - - - -

She's the honey, but the bees
don't know it.

Foul-Mouthed

- - - - - - - - -

His mouth ain't no prayer book.

Mmm, Mmm, Good

Church ladies from around the township held a luncheon at the restaurant where a group of wholesale liquor dealers were eating. At the end of the dealers' lunch, the men ordered a special dessert—watermelon soaked with brandy and rum.

To his horror, the restaurant owner discovered that there had been a mix-up, and the spiked melons had been served by mistake to the church ladies. "Did the women chew you out after they ate the wrong desserts?" he asked the head waiter.

"No, they didn't say a word," the waiter replied. "They was too busy throwin' the seeds from the melons in their purses."

Persistent

- - - - - - - -

She'll stick to it 'til the last pea
is out of the pot.

Clueless

- - - - - - - -

The engine is runnin' but ain't
nobody drivin'.

Honest

If he tells you that rooster
dips snuff, you can look under
its wing and find the can.

Egotistical

He thinks the sun comes up
just to hear him crow.

Elderly

He's two years older than dirt.

Selfish

She's so selfish, she wants the
moon and the sun with two
strands of barbed wire
runnin' 'round 'em.

Unreliable

He sure ain't some boat you'd
tie off to in a storm.

Small

She's littler than a bar of soap
after a week's wash.

Vain

- - - - - - - - -

He breathes through his nose to
keep from wearin' out his teeth.

Squandering

- - - - - - - - -

He's got a taste for champagne
but a billfold for beer.

Gossiping

- - - - - - - - -

She has enough mouth for
ten rows of teeth.

153

Confused

- - - - - - - - - -

He don't know whether to
scratch his watch or wind his butt.

Miserly

- - - - - - - - - -

She's so stingy, she won't
give you the time of day.

Drunk

- - - - - - - - - -

He gets hisself so likkered up
that he could throw himself on
the ground and miss.

Overweight

She wears clothes so tight,
she looks like ten pounds
of potatoes in a five-pound sack.

Dull

He's about as sharp as
mashed potatoes.

Self-Centered

She wouldn't go to a funeral
unless she could be the corpse.

Unattractive

- - - - - - - - -

He's so ugly, his mama took him everywhere so she wouldn't have to kiss him good-bye.

Stupid

- - - - - - - - -

He couldn't pour rain out of a boot if the directions were written on the heel.

Stingy

- - - - - - - - -

He wouldn't pay a nickel to watch an ant pull a freight train.

Blind Faith

At church the other day, a good sister was swaying and dancing in the balcony, when she lost her balance and toppled clear over the railing. But, praise the Lord, her dress caught on the hanging light fixture, leaving her safely suspended but mighty exposed.

Thinking as quick as a rabbit in love, the preacher told the congregation, "The first man who looks at that fine Christian woman will be struck stone blind."

Sitting in the front pew, old Clyde covered half his face, looked up and told himself, "I reckon I can risk one eye."

Squandering

She can spend her paycheck
faster than a preacher can spot
a counterfeit nickel.

Clueless

Not only don't he know nothin',
he don't even suspect nothin'.

Stupid

He was behind the door when
they passed out the brains.

Honest

- - - - - - - -

He's as straight as the
string on a kite.

Dim-Witted

- - - - - - - -

He's three pickles shy of a quart.

Unattractive

He's so ugly, his cooties
have to close their eyes.

Sad

She looks as happy as a
mule with a mouth full
of bumblebees.

Unintelligent

He's as dull as a
widow woman's ax.

Dinner to Die For

A married couple from up north decided to try a restaurant in a small Southern town and dined on fried chicken.

When they finished, the woman told the waitress, "That was simply delicious. Please, miss, would you tell us how you prepare your chickens?"

After a short pause, the waitress replied, "Well, ma'am, around here we don't do anything real special. We just tell 'em straight out: 'You're gonna die.'"

Egotistical

- - - - - - - - -

She thinks she's all that and
a bowl of grits.

Dense

- - - - - - - - -

He acts like he took the late train
and came in on the caboose.

Uptight

- - - - - - - - -

She's wound up tighter than
an eight-day clock.

Corrupt

- - - - - - - - -

He's as crooked as a
barrel full of snakes.

Unattractive

- - - - - - - - -

She ain't exactly ugly. She just
looks better from a distance.

Angry

- - - - - - - - -

He's as mad as a bear with
a sore butt.

Squandering

She spends money faster than
green grass goes through a goose.

Unwanted

He's as welcome as a skunk
at a church picnic.

Useless

He's as useful as a pogo stick
in quicksand.

A Doggone Shame

A traveling salesman drives up
to a cabin in the woods and sees
a barefoot child on the porch
whittling a stick. A hound dog is
laying in the yard.

"Hey, squirt, does your fleabag
bite?" the salesman asks.

The boy replies, "Nope."

So the salesman steps out of his
car. The hound runs over, snarling
and growling, and bites him on
his arms and legs. As the salesman
is flailing around in the dust, he
squeals to the boy, "I thought you
said your dog doesn't bite!"

"It doesn't," said the boy. "But
this here dog ain't mine."

If you want to compliment a cook,
you might say . . .

Boy! That tasted like more!

♦ ♦ ♦

If someone asks about how sick you are,
you might say . . .

I'd have to get better just to die.

♦ ♦ ♦

If someone is trying to con you,
you might say . . .

Don't pee down my leg and tell
me it's rainin'.

When someone is mad at you,
you might say . . .

Who licked the red off your candy?

♦ ♦ ♦

If something seems pointless,
you might say . . .

That juice ain't worth the squeezin'!

♦ ♦ ♦

When it's time to eat, you might say . . .

Let's get greasy 'round the mouth.

♦ ♦ ♦

If you receive some bad news,
you might say . . .

Well, don't that just dill my pickle!

169

*If someone is beating around
the bush, you might say . . .*

Hurry up and get to the
tail of the dog.

♦ ♦ ♦

*If someone tells you something
that you totally agree with,
you might say . . .*

If that ain't the truth, then grits
ain't groceries and eggs
ain't poultry.

♦ ♦ ♦

*If you're explaining something obvious
for the third time, you might say . . .*

You're still lookin' at me like
a calf at a new gate.

170

I'll Drink to That

During a recent hot spell, Uncle Zeke collapses on the street in front of the general store. Several townsfolk rush over to see what they can do.

"Give the poor man a drink of whiskey," a little old lady says.

"Give him some air," says the mailman.

"Give the poor man a drink of whiskey," the elderly woman says again.

"Give him some water," says the schoolteacher.

While several other folks give suggestions, Uncle Zeke sits up and hollers, "Will y'all shut up and listen to the little ol' lady?"

171

When asked if you're going to attend a party, you might say . . .

Yep, if the good Lord's willin' and the creek don't rise.

♦ ♦ ♦

If you're tired of repeating the same thing, you might say . . .

I don't chew my tobacco twice.

♦ ♦ ♦

If you're in an argument with someone who's starting to lose control, you might say . . .

Don't go off with your pistol half-cocked.

*When something is for certain,
you might say . . .*

Is a frog's butt watertight?

♦ ♦ ♦

*When asked how your day is going,
you might say . . .*

As fine as snuff and not
half as dusty.

♦ ♦ ♦

*To a person who makes a statement
that leaves you scratching your head,
you might say . . .*

That makes as much sense as
a trapdoor in a canoe.

173

*If you're talking about a great meal
you just ate, you might say . . .*

That food was so good, it'd make
a body slap his grandma.

♦ ♦ ♦

*If you just hit your thumb with a
hammer, you might say . . .*

It'll feel better when it quits hurtin'.

♦ ♦ ♦

*If someone isn't making much sense,
you might say . . .*

Man, your shirt is missin'
a few buttons.

*If someone came up with a bad idea,
you might say . . .*

That notion will go over like a frog
in the punch bowl.

◆ ◆ ◆

*If you're at a function that has left
you bored, you might say . . .*

I've had fun before, and this ain't it!

◆ ◆ ◆

*If you skipped breakfast and lunch,
you might say . . .*

I'm so hungry, my belly's gonna sue
my teeth for nonsupport.

175

*If you're looking for answers in all the
wrong places, you might say . . .*

I might as well be fishin'
in the clouds.

♦ ♦ ♦

*If you don't have an opinion
while listening to a debate between
other friends, you might say . . .*

I ain't got no dog in this race.

♦ ♦ ♦

*If you come up with a great idea,
you might say . . .*

It's horse high, bull strong, pig
tight, and gooseproof.

If you want to compliment the cook,
you might say . . .

Supper was so good, it makes me
want to swallow my tongue so I can
eat my taste buds.

♦ ♦ ♦

If you have some gossip you want
to dish out, you might say . . .

I'm not one to go 'round spreadin'
rumors, so you better listen close
the first time.

♦ ♦ ♦

If you're in agreement with someone,
you might say . . .

We're both sittin' in amen corner.

In No Hurry

The preacher man meets Moody on the path toward the church, and after exchanging small talk, says, "Do you want to go to heaven?"

Moody's eyes get big and he shakes his head. "No, preacher."

The preacher man is confounded and asks again, "Are you sure you don't want to go to heaven when you die?"

Moody nods this time and says, "Oh, sure, preacher—when I die. I thought you was gettin' a party to go now."

If someone is chewing you out,
you might say . . .

Oh, don't get your tail up and
stinger out!

◆ ◆ ◆

If a friend boasts about completing
a task that most anyone could do,
you might say . . .

It's easy gettin' off a buckin' mule.

◆ ◆ ◆

If your friend tells you that he's being
audited by the IRS, you might say . . .

That'll put a quiver in your liver.

179

When someone gets to the heart of the matter, you might say . . .

You done chewed the bark off the tree.

♦ ♦ ♦

If you find yourself with a serious problem, you might say . . .

Now, ain't this a fine howdy-do.

♦ ♦ ♦

If you don't care one way or the other, you might say . . .

I don't have no knives to sharpen.

In answer to something that's obvious,
you might say . . .

Does a cat have climbin' gear?

♦ ♦ ♦

To someone who is being evasive,
you might say . . .

You're beatin' the devil
'round the stump.

♦ ♦ ♦

If you promise to do something,
but want to leave some wiggle room,
you might say . . .

I'll do it, if nothin' breaks
or comes untwisted.

181

If you're amazed by some unexpected event, you might say . . .

Next thing you know, the hoot owls will be flirtin' with the chickens.

♦ ♦ ♦

If you're sick, you might say . . .

I was better, but I got over it.

♦ ♦ ♦

If you missed lunch, you might say . . .

I'm so hungry, I could eat the south end of a northbound mule.

♦ ♦ ♦

If you are absolutely certain, you might say . . .

As sure as rats run the rafters.

The Right Number

After a few years of home schooling, Johnny shows up for the first time for class at a public school. The teacher explains to him that he can't go to the washroom unless he raises two fingers.

The boy looks puzzled and asks, "Uh, ma'am, how's that gonna stop it?"

If you're ordering someone out of your house, you might say . . .

Don't let the door hit you where the Lord split you.

♦ ♦ ♦

If you want to encourage people to say what they really think, you might say . . .

There's more room out than there is in.

♦ ♦ ♦

If your favorite team won big, you might say . . .

They sure cleaned them boys' plows.

184

If you hear a bad idea, you might say . . .

That makes as much sense as
tryin' to sling a hammock
'tween two cornstalks.

♦ ♦ ♦

*When the family sits down to
a big feast, you might say . . .*

Ya'll be careful now,
or you're gonna fleshen up.

♦ ♦ ♦

*If someone is speaking with great
passion, you might say . . .*

Tell the truth and shame the devil!

Location, Location, Location

The traveling salesman stepped off the train and frowned when he learned that the town was a far piece down the road. "Why in the name of Moses did they put the depot so far from town?" he asked Clinton, one of the locals.

"Well, stranger," said Clinton, "it's probably 'cause they wanted it as close to the tracks as possible."

If a friend is setting unrealistic goals,
you might say . . .

You're hangin' your basket higher
than you can reach.

◆ ◆ ◆

If someone is beating around the bush,
you might say . . .

You're takin' the long way
'round the barn.

◆ ◆ ◆

If a friend is planning to do something
dumb and dangerous, you might say . . .

You might as well pick your teeth
with a rattlesnake.

187

*To emphatically agree with
someone's opinion, you might say . . .*

If that ain't a fact,
God's a possum.

◆ ◆ ◆

*If a friend made a big mistake like
breaking up or quitting a job,
you might say . . .*

You sure dropped your candy.

◆ ◆ ◆

*To a big gossip hound,
you might say . . .*

Keep my name out of your mouth.

When you hear some disturbing news, you might say . . .

Well, that sure jars my preserves!

♦ ♦ ♦

If you're referring to the time you got the last word in an argument, you might say . . .

I sure preached his funeral.

♦ ♦ ♦

If you've overeaten, you might say . . .

I've had more than a plenty.

*If you think someone has the
wrong facts, you might say . . .*

You're sniffin' in the wrong hole.

♦ ♦ ♦

*To someone who has reached the
wrong conclusion, you might say . . .*

You're drivin' your chickens to
the wrong market.

♦ ♦ ♦

*If you're leaving it up to your spouse
to pick a movie, you might say . . .*

Your druthers is my druthers.

*If you really don't feel like going out
with friends, you might say . . .*

I can't dance and it's
too wet to plow.

♦ ♦ ♦

*If you want to compliment someone's
cooking, you might say . . .*

This is gooder 'n grits!

♦ ♦ ♦

*If you need someone to repeat what he
just said, you might say . . .*

Can you lick that calf again?

191

Snake's Alive!

Ol' Bud was catching bass at his favorite fishing hole when he spotted a water moccasin with a frog in its mouth. Bud knew big bass like frogs, so he decided to steal it from the snake.

He sneaked up behind the reptile and grabbed it around the head. Then he pried open the snake's mouth, yanked out the frog, and dropped it in his bait can.

Afraid that the water moccasin would bite him if he let it go, Ol' Bud reached into the back pocket of his bib overalls, pulled out a pint of moonshine, and poured a good amount into the snake's mouth. The water moccasin's eyeballs rolled back and its body went limp. So Bud tossed the snake into the water and went back to fishing.

A few minutes later, Bud felt something rubbing against his bare toe. He looked down and couldn't believe what he was seeing. There was that water moccasin again, only this time it had two frogs in his mouth!

*If you hear something that leaves
you exasperated, you might say . . .*

Well, don't that put pepper in
my gumbo!

♦ ♦ ♦

*If you're getting needled because you're
losing at a game, you might say . . .*

Church ain't over 'til the choir
stops singin'.

♦ ♦ ♦

*If it's time to end the party,
you might say . . .*

Time to pee on the fire and
call in the dogs.

194

Ham-Handed

Fannie goes to see the governor and pleads, "Can you get my husband out of the penitentiary?"

"What's he in for?" the governor asks.

"Stealin' a ham."

"That doesn't sound so bad. Is he a good man?"

"Not really," Fannie admits. "He's a lazy worker and he's mean to me and the kids."

"Then why in blazes do you want a man like that out of prison?"

"'Cause we're out of ham."

*If you're surprised by what you've
just heard, you might say . . .*

Well, pick my peas!

Or

Well, tie me to an anthill
and fill my ears with jam!

Or

Well, tie me to a pig and
roll me in the mud!

Or

Well, don't that cock your pistol!

Or

Well, don't that knock your hat
in the creek!

Or

Well, slap my head and
call me stupid!

Or

Well, don't that put the tassel
on my cap!

Or

Well, butter my butt and
call me a biscuit!

We're continuing to collect country sayings for our annual boxed calendar, *Butter My Butt and Call Me a Biscuit*, which is produced by Andrews McMeel Publishing, LLC, the same company that is publishing this book. If you would like to share your favorite sayings, e-mail them to us at allan@allanzullo.com. If there's a country saying that we haven't heard before and we use it in our next book or calendar, we'll send you a free copy.

◆ ◆ ◆

Allan Zullo, who lives with his wife, Kathryn, on a mountain outside of Asheville, North Carolina, has penned more than ninety nonfiction books. For more information about Allan, go to www.allanzullo.com.

Gene Cheek, a native Carolinian who also lives near Asheville, is the author of the critically acclaimed memoir *The Color of Love*. For more information about Gene, go to www.genecheek.com.